Looking at...

SMOKING

Jillian Powell

WAYLAND

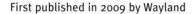

First published in 2009 by Wayland

Wayland
338 Euston Road
London NW1 3BH

Wayland Australia
Level 17/207 Kent Street
Sydney NSW 2000

Produced for Wayland by
White-Thomson Publishing Ltd

+44 (0) 845 362 8240
www.wtpub.co.uk

Editors: Sonya Newland and Katie Powell
Designer: Robert Walster

British Library Cataloguing in Publication Data
  Powell, Jillian
  Looking at smoking
  1. Smoking - Juvenile literature
  I. Title II. Smoking
  362.2'9

ISBN: 9780750258845

Picture Credits
British Museum: 4 (below); Corbis: 21 (Arko
Datta/Reuters); Dreamstime: 12 right (Natie); Eye
Ubiquitous: 6 (Bennett Dean), 8 (John Dakers), 30 top
(David Cumming), 33 (K. Wilton), 35 (Gary Trotter), 42
bottom (Paul Seheult); Getty Images: 29, 37; Sally
Greenhill: 42 top; HWPL: *contents* bottom (Angela
Hampton), 4 top, 7, 9, 12 left, 13 (APM Studios), 19
(Angus Blackburn), 22, 23, 27, 29 (Rupert Horrox), 31
(Angela Hampton), 39, 40 top and bottom, 44; Impact:
28 (Andy Johnstone), 32 top (Caroline Penn), 38 (Ben
Edwards); iStock: *cover*, 11 bottom (Mike Cherim);
James Davis Travel Photography: 17 bottom; Mary
Evans Picture Library: 5; National Film Archive: 10;
Panos Pictures: *contents* top (Giacomo Pirozzi), 11 top;
Quadrant Picture Library: 36; Science Photo Library:
16 (Art Siegel/Custom Medical Stock Photo), 17 top
(Damien Lovegrove), 25 (Colin Cuthbert), 26 bottom
(James Stevenson), 32 bottom (Neil Bromhall); Skjold:
24; South American Pictures: 14 (Tony Morrison),
34 (Rolando Pujol); Roger Vlitos: 15, 20, 26 top, 30
bottom; White-Thomson Publishing Ltd: *title page*,
18, 43, 45.

Printed in China

Wayland is a division of Hachette Children's Books,
an Hachette UK company.
www.hachette.co.uk

CONTENTS

How smoking became popular

Tobacco has been used for thousands of years. People were chewing or smoking the leaves of the tobacco plant long before they understood that tobacco was bad for their health.

↑ Native Americans believed that smoking tobacco could cure everything from toothache to earache.

Tobacco in the Americas

Native Americans smoked peace-pipes of tobacco in religious ceremonies. They also thought it could cure toothache. The Mayan people of Central America smoked tobacco from around AD 500. In 1492, Native Americans gave tobacco to the explorer Christopher Columbus.

→ Native American pipes were works of art. Each man kept his own special pipe.

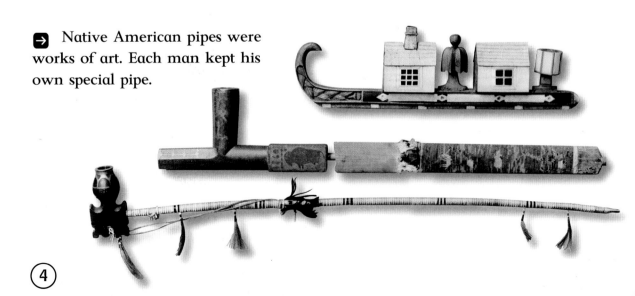

Tobacco in Europe

Tobacco was soon being grown all over Europe. It was sometimes even used instead of money. During the 1700s, it was more popular to take tobacco in the form of snuff. But in the 1800s, the first cigarette factories opened, and cigarettes were produced in large numbers.

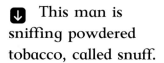
This man is sniffing powdered tobacco, called snuff.

Health warnings

The first health warnings came in 1826, but soldiers in World War I (1914–18) were still given free cigarettes. By the 1920s, smoking was very fashionable. During the 1950s, medical reports began to link smoking with lung cancer.

FACT

People did not really understand that smoking could cause deadly diseases until quite recently. In the 1950s, the first major studies in Britain and the USA linked smoking with lung cancer.

What is tobacco?

Cigarettes, cigars and pipes all contain tobacco. To make cigarettes, the leaves of the tobacco plant are dried, shredded and mixed with chemicals, then rolled in paper. As the tobacco burns, smoke is breathed into the body.

← This boy in Yunnan province, China, is holding dried tobacco leaves.

The effects of nicotine

Smoking makes people feel relaxed because of the drug nicotine, which is in tobacco leaves. When people smoke or chew tobacco, nicotine gets into their bloodstream. When it reaches the smoker's brain it makes them feel good.

'Nicotiana tabacum – the tobacco plant, the most dangerous plant on the planet, currently killing around four million people annually.'

GASP, SMOKE-FREE SOLUTIONS

CASE STUDY ▸ CASE STUDY ▸

Marion has been a smoker nearly all her life. She cannot imagine getting through the day without her cigarettes. She keeps them by her bed so she can have one as soon as she wakes up. She smokes about 40 cigarettes a day.

Marion knows that her cough is caused by smoking, and last year she had to go into hospital because of heart trouble. The doctors told her she was damaging her health and should stop smoking.

Marion knows her health is bad, but she enjoys smoking too much to give up cigarettes. She finds her job boring, and she has lived on her own since getting divorced. She feels she needs her cigarettes just to get through life. Marion tells her doctor she will try to quit smoking, but secretly she feels you have to die of something, and it might as well be something you enjoy.

➡ Marion enjoys her cigarettes and does not want to give them up.

Smoking is a global habit

Today, about a third of all adults worldwide are smokers. In countries such as the UK and the USA, fewer people smoke than they did a few years ago. This is because people are more aware of how it can harm them.

However, in countries such as China, Russia and Poland, the number of smokers is still increasing. China produces and uses more tobacco than any other country. There are more than 300 million Chinese smokers.

'Smoking is falling in developed nations, but in the developing world tobacco consumption is rising by 3.4 per cent per year.'
WORLD HEALTH ORGANIZATION

Smoking and poverty

Poor and unemployed people are most likely to become regular smokers because they feel it helps them escape their problems. Smoking can add to the issues of poverty and disease in some countries. Smokers may choose to buy cigarettes instead of food because they cannot afford both.

➡ In Japan, around 10 per cent of women are smokers. More than half the adult male population smokes.

Environmental issues

Many developing countries grow tobacco to sell to other countries, but they do not grow enough food crops to feed their own people. Tobacco plants need lots of chemical fertilizers, which can spoil the land for food crops.

Huge areas of forest are cut down to make firewood to dry the tobacco leaves. One tree is cut down every fortnight for each person who smokes 20 cigarettes a day.

'Tobacco-growing is a key element of the economy in many developing countries in Africa and South America.'

THE TOBACCO MANUFACTURERS' ASSOCIATION

➡ This Indian man is smoking tobacco through a water-pipe called a hookah.

Becoming a smoker

People start smoking for all different reasons. Most people who are regular smokers start when they are teenagers – sometimes even younger.

The first cigarette

Sometimes people start smoking because they want to find out what it is like. Their first cigarette may make them feel sick, but they see other people enjoying cigarettes and they want to get the same feeling. After a while, they get used to smoking.

⬆ Film stars like Rita Hayworth made smoking look glamorous.

Looking cool

Many people think smoking looks cool or grown-up. All the famous film stars of the 1930s smoked, and their fans wanted to look like them. Seeing film or pop stars smoking makes some people want to do the same, just as they want to dress like them or talk like them.

'Every sleeping and waking hour from billboards, TV screens, movies, radios and now the Internet, the tobacco industry beckons our children.'
WORLD HEALTH ORGANIZATION, TOBACCO-FREE INITIATIVE

Peer pressure

Some people start smoking because their friends are doing it. They are afraid they will be left out if they say they don't want to smoke. If your family or friends smoke, it can feel like the natural thing to do.

Surveys show that children whose family or friends smoke are much more likely to become regular smokers themselves.

⬆ This young Rwandan boy lives on the streets. He begs for money to buy cigarettes and food.

➡ Saying 'no' to cigarettes shows that you know your own mind, and aren't afraid to stand your ground.

Smoking as a comfort

Sometimes people start to smoke when they are feeling worried or under stress. They might have changed schools or jobs. They may have problems at home. They feel they need something to help them deal with the stress. Smoking can help people to concentrate or to relax.

↑ Many smokers start when they are in their early teens. Some start even younger.

↑ Taking exams at school can be stressful and can make people turn to smoking.

FACT

UK surveys show that many people smoke their first cigarette between the ages of nine and 12. In the USA, 60 per cent of smokers start before they are 14 and 90 per cent start before they are 21.

CASE STUDY ▸ CASE STUDY ▸

Leanne started smoking when she was 13, after her grandmother Ellen died. Leanne and her grandmother had been really close. Ellen had been a heavy smoker. When she was 60, she became ill with lung cancer, but she wouldn't give up smoking.

After her grandmother died, Leanne had a hard time at school. She didn't have any close friends and she missed her grandmother a lot. When she started smoking, it felt as if she was getting closer to her grandmother. Everyone was cross with Leanne like they had been with Ellen.

The first time Leanne's mum saw her smoking she was really shocked. She said, 'You're going the same way as your grandmother.'

'I started smoking around the time I changed schools. It was hard to make new friends at first, and everything was strange. Then I got in with a new crowd. They all seemed to smoke, so I did, too. It made me feel like I belonged.'
Dan, 14

➡ Every day people lose loved ones to smoking-related diseases.

Smoking to rebel

Smoking can be a way of rebelling against teachers or parents. Most people know that smoking is bad for you. But smoking can be like wearing a badge that says 'I am old enough to decide for myself'.

Taking risks

Smokers like to feel they can take risks and are not scared of the warnings that are printed on cigarette packets. Taking risks may even be a way of making themselves feel grown-up and in control. This is why one US manufacturer made cigarettes called 'Death'.

'In the young smoker's mind, a cigarette falls into the same category as wine, beer, shaving, wearing a bra — a declaration of independence and striving for self-identity.'

EXTRACT FROM A MARKETING REPORT FOR THE TOBACCO INDUSTRY

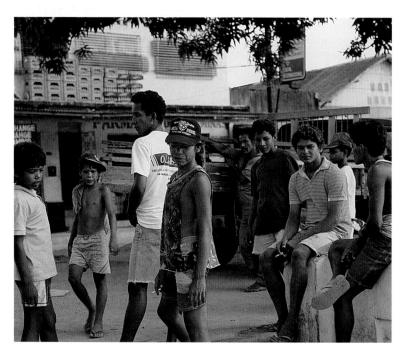

← These children in Brazil are hanging out with teenagers, which can encourage them to start smoking early.

'They are always warning us about something, aren't they? Don't eat this, don't do that. You risk your life every time you cross the road, don't you?'

Nina, 15

← Young people may think it is cool to smoke.

What does smoking say?

• This is my body, OK?

• I can take risks.

• I am a bit of a daredevil.

• I don't mind if my breath and clothes smell of smoke.

• I don't mind spending my money on tobacco.

• I can cope with illness.

FACT

In some Latin American cities, 50 per cent of teenagers smoke. The younger people are when they first start to smoke, the higher their risk of getting lung cancer and other diseases.

Health Education Authority.

'I need a cigarette'

Have you ever heard a smoker say 'I need a cigarette'? Their body is telling them to smoke because it has become addicted to nicotine.

Why is smoking addictive?

Nicotine can calm someone down when they are feeling worried, or it can make them lively if they have been feeling tired.

The nicotine passes into the bloodstream, and reaches the brain in about seven seconds. Once a person has started smoking, their body gets used to nicotine and starts to need it. This is called addiction.

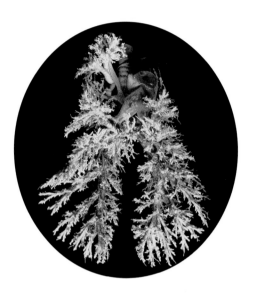

↑ A model of the human lungs. The tiny tubes shown here in pink and white carry nicotine into the bloodstream.

FACT

The drug nicotine is named after Jean Nicot, a courtier who started the fashion for smoking at the French royal court in the sixteenth century.

FACT

Nicotine-replacement products such as gum and patches can help smokers give up. They give low doses of nicotine without the other poisonous chemicals that are in tobacco smoke. These products are less addictive than cigarettes. They help people cope with the craving for nicotine.

↑ Nicotine inhalers give people a low dose of nicotine.

← This young boy in Indonesia feels proud that he is grown-up enough to smoke.

Nicotine is as addictive as heroin

Soon after finishing a cigarette, the amount of nicotine in a smoker's body drops. This can happen even faster if they are eating, or if they are worried or nervous. They start to feel jumpy and can't relax. Soon they need to smoke another cigarette to feel better again.

Nicotine is as addictive as the drug heroin. As a person's body gets used to nicotine, they need to smoke more often. They may need to smoke every 20 to 45 minutes to keep up the level of nicotine in their blood.

'A cigarette is a carefully crafted product that delivers just the right amount of nicotine to keep its user addicted for life before killing the person.'

DR GRO HARLEM BRUNDTLAND, WORLD HEALTH ORGANIZATION

← Some people chain-smoke − they light their next cigarette from the one they are already smoking.

Getting hooked

It is easy to get hooked on cigarettes. People often start by smoking occasionally when they are out with friends. Then they may find they fancy a cigarette when they are on their own, so they start to buy packets themselves. Once people buy their own cigarettes, they are likely to smoke more.

'Smoking a cigarette for the beginner is a symbolic act. "I am no longer my mother's child, I am tough, I am an adventurer..." But as the power of this idea fades away, the chemical effects of the drug take over, and the smoker gets hooked.'

ADAPTED FROM A QUOTE FROM THE VICE-PRESIDENT FOR RESEARCH AND DEVELOPMENT, CIGARETTE MANUFACTURER PHILIP MORRIS

← This young woman sits down to relax with a magazine and a cigarette.

The smoking habit

Addiction means that the smoker's body needs nicotine. It also means that the person has started to rely on cigarettes to get through stressful times. Smoking quickly becomes a habit. Habits can be comforting and help us feel in control. Smokers get used to the feeling of a cigarette in their hand or mouth. Cigarettes become part of their daily routine.

'Smoking is just part of being me. When I go out clubbing, I take my make-up, enough money for the club and a taxi, and my cigarettes. What else do you do while you are waiting for your friends to turn up?'
SHELLEY, 17

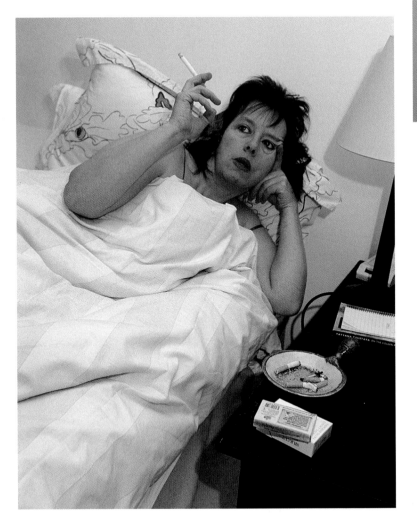

More than one-third of smokers light up in the first 15 minutes of the day.

CASE STUDY ▸ CASE STUDY ▸ CASE STUDY ▸ CASE STUDY ▸

Rajeema has smoked for years. When she is at work, Rajeema has to go and stand outside the building to have a cigarette. Some of her workmates come too and they enjoy a chat and a smoke.

Rajeema also smokes when she is out with her friends. It stops her feeling shy when she meets someone new. People are always handing round cigarettes and smoking makes Rajeema feel part of the crowd.

Rajeema's friend Jamila would like to give up because she wants to save money to get married next year, but it's hard saying no all the time. Sometimes, the boys make fun of Jamila because she doesn't want to smoke. Rajeema feels sorry for Jamila, but Jamila is determined to give up.

← Many smokers use coffee and lunch breaks to have a cigarette.

When do people smoke?

Some people have a cigarette as soon as they wake up in the morning. Others smoke with a cup of coffee or after a meal. Cigarettes can also help people feel relaxed at parties, or when they meet new people for the first time.

The risks of smoking

Some people say that everything in life is a risk, but there are some risks you can avoid – such as smoking.

What are the risks?

There are over 4,000 chemicals and gases in the smoke from a burning cigarette. Many of them are poisonous. They include:

- Carbon monoxide, which is a gas found in car exhaust fumes.

- Nicotine.

- Sticky black tar.

- Poisonous metals such as arsenic.

↑ Thousands of poisonous chemicals are released when a cigarette burns.

When someone smokes a cigarette, smoke passes along the bronchial tubes leading to their lungs. These tubes are lined with tiny hairs that keep dirt and germs out of the lungs. Smoke damages the hairs so the tubes cannot keep out dirt and germs so well.

Effects inside the body

Nicotine makes the heart beat faster and raises the blood pressure. Carbon monoxide makes it harder for the blood to carry oxygen round the body.

Soot and tar stick to the lungs. This can cause coughing and breathing problems. It can also lead to lung diseases such as lung cancer.

⬇ A poster showing the dangers of tar.

FACT

Smoking causes 90 per cent of deaths from lung cancer worldwide. Tobacco use is estimated to cause 20 per cent of all deaths worldwide.

WORLD HEALTH ORGANIZATION.

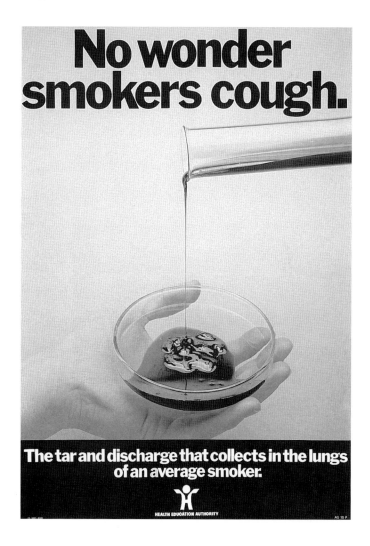

No wonder smokers cough.

The tar and discharge that collects in the lungs of an average smoker.

HEALTH EDUCATION AUTHORITY

Future health

Four times as many people die from smoking as they do from other risky pastimes such as drinking alcohol or taking drugs. But to many people, the risks of smoking do not seem real.

When we are young, illnesses in later life may seem too far ahead to worry about. But people who did not worry when they were young are today facing long illnesses.

FACT

Worldwide, four million people a year die from smoking-related diseases. By 2030, this figure is expected to rise to 10 million.

WORLD HEALTH ORGANIZATION.

'Virtually every activity involves some potential risk, whether it be smoking, skiing, swimming or driving a car.'

US TOBACCO COMPANY, PHILIP MORRIS

← Cigarette makers sometimes compare smoking with other risky but enjoyable pastimes such as windsurfing. Yet most sports improve rather than damage our health.

CASE STUDY ▸ CASE STUDY ▸ CASE STUDY ▸ CASE STUDY ▸

For 20 years, Sheila made the same New Year's resolution to give up smoking, but each time she failed. She was smoking 40 a day, and even when she lost her job as a shop manager, and had little money, she carried on smoking. If anything, she smoked more when she was out of a job.

Then Sheila found she had lung cancer. She had to have weeks of chemotherapy and radiotherapy. She lost her hair and felt tired and sick most of the time. Sheila's treatment can't cure her because the cancer has spread.

Sheila has two teenage sons. Some of their friends are already smokers. Sheila knows that her boys may start smoking, because she took it up even though her own mum had died of cancer. Somehow, she felt it would never happen to her because she had always felt healthy until recently.

← Cancer patients may need to take strong drugs, which can cause side-effects, such as making their hair fall out.

'A cigarette is the only freely available consumer product, which, when regularly consumed as indicated, kills.'
WORLD HEALTH ORGANIZATION

The physical cost

If you smoke, your breath, hair and clothes may smell of stale tobacco smoke. Tar and nicotine make your teeth look yellow or grey, and tar stains your fingers yellow.

Even young smokers may show signs of ageing as early as their twenties. Their skin may look dull and lines may form around their mouth and eyes.

This young smoker already has wrinkles.

The health cost

Smokers are less fit than non-smokers. They get out of breath quickly when they exercise. Many smokers have coughs because their body is trying to clear their lungs. They usually have more health problems than non-smokers.

We can tell that this man is a smoker because his fingers and nails are stained by tar.

'I didn't think I smelt of smoke. I have always been really careful about cleaning my teeth properly and things like that. It really upset me when I kissed this girl and she told me my breath smelt like an ashtray!'
JOSH, 19

FACT

From 1950 to 2000, around 62 million people died
from diseases caused by smoking. That is more
than all the people killed during World War II.

WORLD HEALTH ORGANIZATION.

⬇ This girl suffers
from a morning cough,
as her lungs try to
clear themselves.

The financial cost

Smoking is also a very expensive
habit. Experts have estimated that
someone who starts smoking when
they are 20 years old will end up
spending around £100,000 on
cigarettes throughout their life.

'Cigarette smoking is now as
important a cause of death as
were the great epidemic diseases
such as typhoid, cholera and
tuberculosis that affected previous
generations in this country.'

THE BRITISH ROYAL COLLEGE OF PHYSICIANS

Living and working with smokers

Some people think that smokers should be able to smoke wherever they want. But now we know more about the risks of passive smoking, do non-smokers have a right to clean air?

Passive smoking

Passive smoking means breathing in someone else's cigarette smoke. Being in a smoky room can give some people coughs, red eyes, sore throats, headaches and breathing problems. Non-smokers can even get serious diseases such as lung cancer if they are around smokers a lot.

'After I have been to work, the next morning I am coughing like a smoker. I used to think it wasn't worth quitting because working in a bar is as bad as smoking.'

NICOLE, BARTENDER AND WAITRESS

➡ Around 40 per cent of adults in France are smokers. It is hoped that the ban on smoking in public places, introduced in 2007, will reduce this.

➡ In many countries smokers now have to go outside for a cigarette.

> 'Even if smokers are in a minority, their needs should still be catered for.'
>
> TOBACCO MANUFACTURERS' ASSOCIATION

Smoking bans

In Europe and the USA, smoking is now banned in many public places, such as cinemas, bars and restaurants. If people want to smoke they have to go outside.

FACT

In the USA, research has shown that around 3,800 people a year die from lung cancer caused by passive smoking. Bar and restaurant workers are one and a half times more likely to get lung cancer than the rest of the population.

US ENVIRONMENTAL PROTECTION AGENCY, IN A REPORT RELEASED BEFORE THE BAN ON SMOKING IN PUBLIC PLACES.

In a lot of places people are not allowed to smoke inside offices. Companies are afraid that they might be taken to court if employees get ill from passive smoking.

Children's health

Nearly half the children in the world live in the same house as a smoker. Children who live with smokers are more likely to get coughs, colds and illnesses such as bronchitis. They get tired more easily because of the poisonous chemicals in their blood.

If both parents smoke, children can suffer even more. They can passively smoke the same as 80 cigarettes a year. Even pets can have breathing problems.

⬆ The child of a smoker, such as this baby in Indonesia, is twice as likely to become a smoker himself as the child of a non-smoker.

⬅ Pets can suffer health problems from passive smoking, too.

CASE STUDY ▶ CASE STUDY ▶ CASE STUDY ▶ CASE STUDY ▶

Carol started smoking when she was 14. Although she cut down when her children were born, she carried on smoking. As her family grew, she tried not to smoke around her children, especially when they had colds or infections.

Carol had heard of asthma, but she didn't know much about it until the doctor said that her 10-year-old daughter, Angharad, and nine-year-old son, Liam, were both asthmatic. Carol's doctor warned her that passive smoking would make the children's breathing problems worse. Carol tried not to smoke when the children were home from school, but she still enjoyed having a cigarette when she was watching television, or after a meal.

When Liam was 11, he had a really bad asthma attack and had to be rushed to hospital. Carol knew she had to stop smoking completely, not just for her own health but also for the sake of the children.

'The anti-smoking lobby won't rest until smoking is banned in every place of work, including pubs, clubs and restaurants for which smokers represent a substantial part of their business.'

SIMON CLARK, DIRECTOR OF FOREST, FOR SMOKERS' RIGHTS

◀ This boy is using a spacer to inhale his asthma medicine. Breathing in tobacco smoke can cause an asthma attack.

Risks to unborn children

If a woman smokes when she is pregnant, her baby becomes a passive smoker. The mother passes all the poisonous chemicals in cigarettes to her baby through her bloodstream. The baby does not grow as much as it should. There is a danger that the baby could be born prematurely or stillborn.

Risks to pregnant women

Pregnant women who smoke are more likely to get ill and have to go into hospital. It can be hard for a pregnant woman to quit, though. They might be worrying about money or relationships, or what will happen once the baby is born. They may smoke to relax.

↑ Being pregnant can be stressful, so some women smoke even though they know the risks to their baby.

← A 20-week-old baby boy in the womb. He may already be passively smoking.

Reducing the risks

About two-thirds of women who smoke give up when they get pregnant. Others cut down the number of cigarettes they smoke. They may inhale more deeply when they do smoke, but this is not always the case.

If a woman stops smoking before she falls pregnant, or in the early months, she can reduce the risks to herself and her baby.

FACT

A smoker's baby weighs an average 200 grams less than a non-smoker's. Smaller babies are more likely to become ill.

'I'd been a smoker for six years before I got pregnant. I'd tried giving up before, but once I knew about the baby, I stopped just like that. I didn't want to take any risks with my baby.'

DEBBIE, 24

← Women who choose not to smoke in pregnancy give their baby a good start in life.

The profits from tobacco

Tobacco makes a lot of money for the people who grow and sell it. Tobacco farmers, manufacturers, shopkeepers and governments all benefit from the tobacco industry.

Tobacco farming

Tobacco is grown in about 100 countries around the world. Often farmers can make more money from growing tobacco than from food crops. In countries such as Venezuela, tobacco manufacturers sometimes give tobacco farmers money to help with farming technology.

'Every time someone buys tobacco products, they are supporting an industry that goes for profit before people, without regard for human suffering or environmental cost.'

GASP, SMOKE-FREE SOLUTIONS

→ These farmers are harvesting tobacco leaves on a farm in Cuba.

Tobacco companies

International tobacco companies are among the richest in the world. In the USA, more money is made in the tobacco industry than in the computer industry. But nowadays, fewer people in developed countries are buying cigarettes. Also, some people have taken the tobacco companies to court because they have become ill from smoking cigarettes.

⬆ These men in a café in Cairo, Egypt, are smoking a hookah, which often contains a lot of tar and nicotine.

New markets

Because of this, tobacco companies have started selling more cigarettes in developing countries in South America, the Middle East, Africa and Asia. The tobacco companies still make a lot of money, but now it comes from different parts of the world.

Cigarette advertising

Cigarette manufacturers spend millions of pounds every year to make people aware of their brands. In some countries, tobacco companies sponsor sports events to make people aware of their brands of cigarettes. They also advertise by paying film-makers to show film stars smoking their brand. In many places, though, this kind of advertising is no longer allowed.

'There is no convincing evidence that tobacco advertising causes anybody — adult or child — to start smoking.'

TOBACCO
MANUFACTURERS'
ASSOCIATION

Encouraging smoking

Some people say that it is wrong to encourage people to take up smoking. The tobacco industry argues that it is not trying to encourage new smokers, but to persuade people who already smoke to switch brands.

➡ Cigarette companies used to advertise on Formula One cars, but laws in many countries now forbid this.

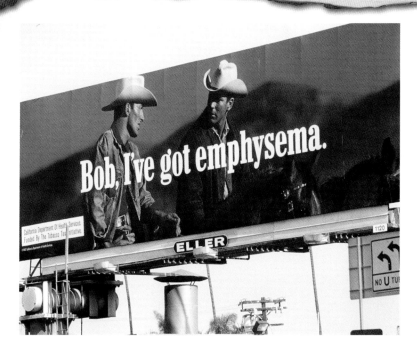

Some groups used anti-smoking posters to try and get laws passed against advertising cigarettes. Advertising on billboards is now banned.

Advertising bans

In 1998, the European Union passed a law to ban advertising on television, radio and on billboards. In 2003, it stopped companies calling cigarettes 'mild' or 'light'. It said this made people think such cigarettes were safe to smoke.

In 2005, the World Health Organization passed a treaty called the Framework Convention on Tobacco Control. This had lots of laws about how tobacco should be controlled. It included a law that said all tobacco advertising must be banned.

'The tobacco companies make you believe that if you smoke, you're going to be sexy, attractive, successful, accepted by your peers. They project this image in every media — from daytime movies to night-time movies, magazines and even cartoons.'

ALLEN LANDERS, TOBACCO CONTROL ACTIVIST

Who benefits?

Governments earn billions of pounds in taxes every year from the tobacco industry. In Denmark, 84 per cent of the price of a packet of cigarettes is tax. The British Government received around £8.5 billion in tax from the tobacco industry in 2005.

Who pays?

Every year, billions of pounds are spent on caring for smokers who have become ill. Millions of working days are lost, too, which costs companies a lot of money.

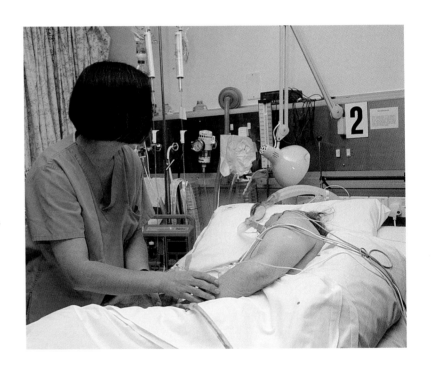

↑ Many smokers will end up spending a lot of time in hospital.

'The tobacco industry is a major contributor to the UK economy. [In one year] it would, for example, pay for three-quarters of the Education and Employment budget.'

THE TOBACCO MANUFACTURERS' ASSOCIATION

More companies are now becoming aware of the costs to their businesses and their workers of illnesses caused by smoking. Some now have schemes to encourage employees to quit.

CASE STUDY ▸ CASE STUDY ▸ CASE STUDY ▸ CASE STUDY ▸

Last year Jamie was off sick from his job in Glasgow for a total of 30 days. Jamie is a heavy smoker. He has always suffered with a bad chest, and even a cold or flu can leave him unwell for several weeks. Recently, Jamie has begun to have pains in his chest and arms. Doctors have told him he has heart trouble, made worse by his smoking habit. Jamie's employers have always allowed their staff to smoke, but now they are considering a no-smoking policy at work. Every year they lose hundreds of working days because of illness among their staff.

A report into smoking in the workplace by the Scottish Health Education Board found that smokers take almost one-third more sick leave every year than non-smokers.

← Another day off work because of illness.

Quitting the habit

Most smokers decide at some time that they would like to give up. They may be worried about their health, or need to stop spending money on cigarettes.

Wanting to quit

Smokers must really want to give up if they are going to succeed. Some fail because they don't want to give up enough. Some may feel they cannot cope without their cigarettes. Others say they are giving up, but think it will be alright if they have a cigarette now and again.

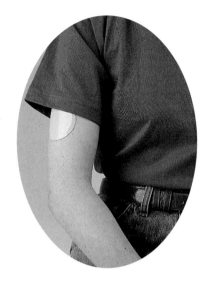

Nicotine patches deliver nicotine into the bloodstream through the skin to stop the craving for cigarettes.

Chewing gum can help smokers to quit by giving them small amounts of nicotine.

Withdrawal symptoms

The first days or weeks after giving up can be hard because the body has become used to nicotine. People may have headaches and feel nervous and jumpy. They might feel dizzy or find it hard to sleep. They have cravings for a cigarette, especially when under stress.

⬇ There are now several aids to help people stop smoking, including tablets, gum and nicotine inhalers.

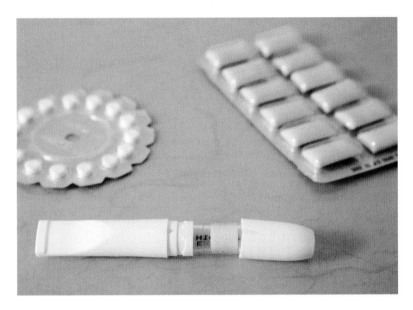

Quitting aids

Some smokers try nicotine gum or patches to help them get through the first weeks. Others get help from a counsellor or join a no-smoking group, where everyone supports each other.

FACT

54 per cent of smokers in Britain say they want to quit. Around 1,000 people a day manage to quit smoking.

QUIT.

Hints for quitting:

- Cut down smoking gradually, or...

- Stop on a particular day, such as New Year's Day.

- Keep a smoker's diary, when the smoker writes down when they most want a cigarette and thinks of other things to do instead.

- Take up exercise.

- Eat healthy food instead of smoking.

⬆ A healthy diet and exercise will help an ex-smoker stay in shape.

Weight control

Some people worry that they will put on weight when they stop smoking. This is because people tend to eat more when they are quitting. Food also tastes better if you don't smoke.

Ex-smokers may find that their weight increases slightly, but it usually settles after a little while.

⬅ Being a non-smoker is part of living a healthy life.

CASE STUDY ▸ CASE STUDY ▸ CASE STUDY ▸ CASE STUDY ▸

John is in his early forties. He started smoking when he became a lorry driver in his twenties. He smoked about 50 cigarettes a day. When he got home, John always felt too tired to exercise, until his partner Sandra bought a puppy. John started taking the dog for long walks at the weekends.

It was then that John began getting bad pains in his legs. He went to the doctor, who told him that his blood had become thick and sticky. There was a risk that John could lose his legs, or even die. John knew that his only chance was to give up smoking and get fitter. It was hard because he had always had a packet of cigarettes in his cab.

John got used to smoking a dummy cigarette and used nicotine skin patches to help him over the first few weeks. Now he has stopped smoking altogether. When he feels like having a cigarette, he takes the dog out instead.

➡ Getting out and about can make it easier to quit.

Feeling healthy again

Smokers who give up understand the health risks and what it means to be addicted to a drug like nicotine. They know that even if they feel bad when they first give up, they will soon start to feel better.

'If you want to stop smoking, any method can help. If you don't want to stop, no method will help.'

THE HEALTH EDUCATION AUTHORITY

⬇ Non-smokers have more money to spend on things they enjoy; these boys saved up for their bikes.

Long-term benefits

When smokers quit, they begin to feel fitter and less breathless when they exercise. Ex-smokers find that their teeth and fingers gradually lose the tar stains. After a few months the lungs start to clear and work properly. After about 15 years, an ex-smoker has the same risk of early death as a non-smoker.

'My life has changed dramatically. I feel that smoking is not worth it anymore and I just wouldn't swap the benefits of quitting.'

SARAH, WINNER OF QUIT's AWARD FOR UK QUITTER OF THE YEAR, 2004

← Choosing not to smoke is a lifestyle choice, like choosing to do sports or get fit.

'When you've given up smoking and you have a craving, you have to understand what's going on in your head. When I want a cigarette I think, "Wouldn't it be awful to go through all that again?" For one cigarette it's just not worth it.'

LAUREN, EX-SMOKER

GLOSSARY

Addiction

When a person has a desperate need for something, such as a drug, and cannot give it up without help.

Asthma

An illness that causes breathing problems.

Bronchial

To do with the lungs.

Bronchitis

A disease that makes the air tubes in the lungs swell up.

Cancer

A disease that can affect all different parts of the body. Smokers are at risk of lung cancer in particular.

Carbon monoxide

A poisonous gas contained in cigarettes that gets into the smoker's bloodstream.

Chain-smoker

Someone who smokes so much that they often light up a cigarette from the one they are already smoking.

Chemotherapy

The treatment of disease, especially cancer, using chemical substances.

Cravings

The strong need or desire for something.

Dependence

When someone feels they have to keep taking a drug, such as nicotine, to feel okay or to avoid feeling bad.

Emphysema

A disease that damages the lungs and causes breathing problems.

Epidemic disease

A disease that spreads very widely among people in an area at a certain time.

Heroin

A very addictive drug made from morphine that is usually injected by users.

Inhale

To breathe in, for example, air or tobacco smoke.

Nicotine

A chemical in cigarettes that makes smokers keep wanting to smoke.

Passive smoking

Breathing in other people's cigarette smoke.

Premature

Too early; before the normal time.

Quit

To give something up.

Radiotherapy

The treatment of cancer and other diseases using X-rays.

Snuff

Tobacco that is sniffed through the nose.

Sponsor

To support a sports or arts event as a way of advertising a product.

Stillborn

When a baby is born dead.

Tar

A dark, thick substance in tobacco. Different brands of cigarette have different amounts of tar, so they are labelled high-tar or low-tar.

Withdrawal

How the body reacts when a drug that someone has become dependent on is no longer taken.

FURTHER INFORMATION

ORGANIZATIONS

UK

ASH (Action on Smoking
and Health)
First Floor
144–145 Shoreditch High Street
London E1 6JE
Tel: 0207 739 5902
www.ash.org.uk
Campaigns for policies to
control the health problems
caused by tobacco.

FOREST (Freedom Organization
for the Right to Enjoy Smoking
Tobacco)
Sheraton House
Castle Park
Cambridge CB3 0AX
Tel: 01223 370156
www.forestonline.org
Campaigns for smokers' rights.

GASP Smoke-free Solutions
93 Cromwell Road
Bristol BS6 5EX
Tel: 0117 955 0101
www.gasp.org.uk
Resources on tobacco control and
smoking education.

Health Development Agency
MidCity Place
71 High Holborn
London WC1V 6NA
Tel: 0845 003 7780
www.nice.org.uk
Part of the National Institute for
Health and Clinical Excellence.

QUIT
211 Old Street
London EC1V 9NR
Tel: 020 7251 1551
www.quit.org.uk
Smokers Quitline 0800 00 22 00
Helps smokers quit.

WDM (World Development
Movement)
66 Offley Road
London SW9 0LS
Tel: 020 7820 4900
www.wdm.org.uk
Campaigns against tobacco
use and promotion in the
developing world.

USA

ASH (Action on Smoking
and Health)
2013 H Street NW
Washington, D.C. 20006
Tel: (202) 659 4310
www.ash.org

Americans for Nonsmoker's Rights
2530 San Pablo Ave
Suite J, Berkeley
California 94702
Tel: (510) 841 3032
www.no-smoke.org

Office on Smoking and Health
at Centers for Disease Control
Mail Stop K-50
4770 Buford Highway NE
Atlanta, Georgia 30341-3742
www.cdc.gov/tobacco

FURTHER READING

*Know the Facts: Drinking and
Smoking*
by Paul Mason
(Wayland, 2008)

Health Issues: Smoking
by Sally Morgan
(Wayland, 2003)

It's your Health: Smoking
by J. Anderson
(Franklin Watts, 2004)

Choices and Decisions: Smoking
by Peter Saunders and Stephen
Myers
(Franklin Watts, 2004)

INDEX